STRONG, HEALTHY GIRLS

EARNING AN INCOME

By Rebecca J. Allen

CONTENT CONSULTANT

Dr. Amy Bellmore
Professor of Human Development
University of Wisconsin–Madison

Essential Library

An Imprint of Abdo Publishing | abdobooks.com

abdobooks.com

Published by Abdo Publishing, a division of ABDO, PO Box 398166, Minneapolis, Minnesota 55439. Copyright © 2021 by Abdo Consulting Group, Inc. International copyrights reserved in all countries. No part of this book may be reproduced in any form without written permission from the publisher. Essential Library™ is a trademark and logo of Abdo Publishing.

Printed in the United States of America, North Mankato, Minnesota.
082020
012021

THIS BOOK CONTAINS
RECYCLED MATERIALS

Cover Photo: iStockphoto
Interior Photos: Iana Chyrva/iStockphoto, 8; iStockphoto, 10, 32, 37, 44–45, 56; Juan Monino/iStockphoto, 14–15, 80–81; SDI Productions/iStockphoto, 16, 39; Lise Gagne/iStockphoto, 20; Robin J Gentry/Shutterstock Images, 23; Olena Yakobchuk/Shutterstock Images, 25, 28–29; Shutterstock Images, 34, 50–51, 66, 74–75, 83, 92–93; MangoStar Studio/iStockphoto, 42; Lisa F. Young/Shutterstock Images, 48; Africa Studio/Shutterstock Images, 52; Praetorian Photo/iStockphoto, 59; Leonel Manzanarez/Shutterstock Images, 60; Odua Images/Shutterstock Images, 63; Ermolaev Alexander/Shutterstock Images, 68–69; Monkey Business Images/Shutterstock Images, 70–71; Lewis Tse Pui Lung/iStockphoto, 78; Dmytro Zinkevych/Shutterstock Images, 84–85; Olena Zaskochenko/Shutterstock Images, 87; Liudmyla Supynska/iStockphoto, 90; Yakobchuk Viacheslav/Shutterstock Images, 97; PR Image Factory/Shutterstock Images, 98

Editor: Megan Ellis
Series Designer: Nikki Nordby

Library of Congress Control Number: 2019954373
Publisher's Cataloging-in-Publication Data

Names: Allen, Rebecca J, author.
Title: Earning an income / by Rebecca J. Allen
Description: Minneapolis, Minnesota : Abdo Publishing, 2021 | Series: Strong, healthy girls | Includes online resources and index.
Identifiers: ISBN 9781532192166 (lib. bdg.) | ISBN 9781098210069 (ebook)
Subjects: LCSH: Money-making projects for girls--Juvenile literature. | Personal budgets--Juvenile literature. | Personal income--Juvenile literature. | Social skills in adolescence--Juvenile literature. | Responsibility in adolescence--Juvenile literature.
Classification: DDC 155.533--dc23

CONTENTS

MEET

DR. AMY

Dr. Amy Bellmore is fascinated by humans and inspired by teens. She works as a professor of human development in the Department of Educational Psychology at the University of Wisconsin–Madison, where she conducts research on the peer relationships of adolescents and teaches courses on adolescent development.

She earned a PhD in developmental psychology at the University of Connecticut. Though she did not declare a major in psychology until the middle of her sophomore year in college, she has evidence that she was destined to study teens from a work aptitude test she took her sophomore year in high school. Based on the results of the test about her interests and skills, she discovered that the best job for her was a research psychologist. Now that she has worked in that career for almost twenty years, she is happy to verify that the test was correct.

During her career, Dr. Amy has conducted numerous studies on the social experiences of teens, which are published in more than sixty articles and book chapters. Most of these studies take place through partnerships with public middle schools and high schools across Wisconsin that share the goal of promoting the welfare of adolescents. Following the leads of the teens themselves, who have moved parts of their lives to online spaces, Dr. Amy's most recent research attends to the ways teens use social media to create and maintain their social relationships. Dr. Amy loves using social media herself, and she finds this research area particularly exciting because teens create and transform technology in new and different ways. Dr. Amy also serves as an associate editor for the *Journal of Research on Adolescence*, which is the flagship journal for the Society of Research on Adolescence, a community of researchers dedicated to the well-being of adolescents.

In her nonwork life, Dr. Amy stays on the pulse of youth culture (and generally enjoys rocking out) by regularly attending concerts of pop-culture icons. Dr. Amy splits her time between Madison, Wisconsin, and Los Angeles, California, with her adolescent puggles, Presley and Riddock.

TAKE IT

FROM ME

If you've picked up this book, there's a good chance you're thinking about applying for your first job. In fact, many teens are interested in getting a job and earning an income. In May 2019, almost five million 16- to 19-year-olds, or 29 percent of people in that age group, had jobs.

Maybe you'd like money to buy a new video game. Maybe you want to start saving for college or your first apartment. Maybe you want an early start developing your résumé or getting work experience. Whatever your motivation, this book will help you think through which types of jobs are available, and more importantly, which type of job you want. It will also alert you to some challenges you may face while you pursue your goals.

One of the best ways to start your job search is to think about something that interests you. Your ideal job might be scooping ice cream at the shop down the street (free ice cream!) or working in a veterinarian's office (time with furry friends!). You could also start by thinking about the questions you have about your job search. Who would hire you? What would your responsibilities be? What will your boss expect?

It's OK to be nervous about getting a job. The good news is that most people have some way of earning an income, so most people have gone through this process before. Many companies need people to help them get work done. So if the first position you apply for isn't a good fit, move on to the next company on your list. The right job for you is out there—you just need to find it.

ALL THE BEST!
REBECCA

CHAPTER ONE

A BIT MORE MONEY

As you think about earning an income, certain jobs may immediately jump out at you. Maybe you love talking to other people. You may see a grocery store cashier, a host at a pizza restaurant, or a salesperson in a department store and think that these positions would be good fits. If you like spending time with children, you may want to work at a tutoring center or public park. These jobs would require you to talk to customers or visitors regularly.

However, not everyone feels comfortable talking to others! Some jobs don't require you to interact with other people as often. If you like working alone and setting your own pace, you might consider jobs such as shelving books at the library, working at a greenhouse, or stocking shelves at a grocery store. These jobs might be better fits for your skills, interests, or personality.

Another thing to consider is the amount of time that you'd like to work at your job. Some jobs are part-time, which generally means working fewer than 40 hours every week. Part-time jobs could include working in a restaurant, coffee shop, or retail store. Other jobs are seasonal, which means they are only available over the summer or during winter holidays. You may work a lot of hours during a seasonal position, but the job only lasts for a short period of time. Some types of seasonal jobs include camp

counselor, greenhouse worker, lifeguard, or store cashier during the holiday shopping season.

Before beginning your job search, talk to your friends or classmates about their jobs. What do they like about them? What don't they like? Their answers might help you picture the type of work you'd really enjoy. They could also help you figure out which types you *wouldn't* enjoy. You could also speak to teachers, neighbors, or anyone who might know about jobs for teens or work in a field you'd like to learn about. They may know about a position that's perfect for you or be able to refer you to an employer.

Let's see how Clarissa figured out which part-time job might be a good fit for her skills and interests.

CLARISSA'S STORY

Clarissa sat at the lunch table, pushing soggy peas around her plate. Her friend Violet's phone had just vibrated with a new text, and now Violet's attention was glued to the screen.

Clarissa's beat-up iPhone stayed tucked in her backpack at school unless she absolutely needed it. It was her mom's old phone—a hand-me-down with a cracked screen. It didn't even have cellular service, so Clarissa could only use it at places with free Wi-Fi. Thanks to that, Clarissa knew all the places in town where she could access free Wi-Fi if she ever needed to send a quick message.

= **What are your interests?**

= **What skills do you want to use in your job?**

= **What type of environment do you want to work in? Retail? An office? Outdoors?**

= **What type of people do you want as coworkers?**

What could she even put on her résumé when she'd never had a job?

Clarissa wanted a new phone, but her mother said she could have one only if she saved up the money herself. Unfortunately, even a low-end smartphone would cost at least $100. To Clarissa, who received money on certain holidays only, it might as well have been a few million dollars. She knew that she needed a job to save up the money for a new phone.

As Clarissa thought about her situation, she started smashing peas with her fork. Getting a job seemed difficult. She'd heard about things like résumés, cover letters, and interviews, but she didn't even know where to start. What could she even put on her résumé when she'd never had a job?

Then again, Clarissa knew other people in her grade who had jobs. Violet worked at the neighborhood pool as a lifeguard, and Clarissa knew that it had been her first job. She had shifts two days a week after school and one day on the weekend.

Clarissa couldn't be a lifeguard, though. She wasn't a strong enough swimmer— she could only dog-paddle. Plus, she didn't like the idea of working after school. With student government and prom committee taking up a lot of her after-school time, she'd need to work on the weekends instead.

As she smashed more peas on her plate, she got an idea. Maybe a job with food would be a good fit. The convenience store around the corner from her house had a help wanted sign pretty much permanently affixed to its door. There was also Luigi's Pizza next to the library. The restaurant had an amazing smell that hit you when you opened the door: tomatoes, Italian spices, and cheesy goodness. It made Clarissa long for pizza even when she'd just finished lunch. That would be a great fit, especially since it probably included free slices of pizza!

Violet finally put her phone facedown on the table and turned to Clarissa again. "Sorry about that," she said. "Someone needed me to cover their shift at the pool tonight."

"No problem," Clarissa said. "I was just thinking—how did you decide to take the job at the pool? Is it hard to manage your work

TALK ABOUT IT

= What kinds of jobs do the people around you have?

= When could you work? Right after school? Evenings? Weekends?

= How would you get to work? Walk? Ride your bike? Take the bus? Drive?

= How far away from school and home could you work without the commute taking too much time?

hours and all your homework? If I want a job, how do I get one?"

Violet's eyes went wide. "Whoa. When did you get so serious about getting a job?"

Clarissa laughed. "I'm not sure I'm so serious about getting a job, but I'm definitely serious about making some money."

Violet nodded. "I hear you, but you don't want just any job. If you have to give up your Saturdays and stay up later to get homework done, you'd better like what you're doing."

> "I'm not sure I'm so serious about getting a job, but I'm definitely serious about making some money."

"That makes sense," Clarissa said.

"I got my job at the pool because I knew I liked swimming, and that was pretty much my only reason for applying there," Violet said. "But then after lifeguard training and learning all about first responders, I'm considering a career as a paramedic or firefighter."

Clarissa was shocked. "Seriously? But you've been talking about being a vet since like second grade."

Violet laughed. "I know, but last summer when I volunteered at the animal shelter, it was really difficult to look at the sad dogs

TALK ABOUT IT

= What are some jobs that would be interesting or fun in addition to providing a paycheck?

= Which activities are you willing to give up to make time for work?

= Can you afford to *not* get a job?

every single day and not take all of them home. I've really enjoyed lifeguarding though, and it'd be nice to help those in need—just people instead of pets!"

Now it was Clarissa's turn to laugh. "Got it," she said.

She started thinking about Luigi's Pizza again. Maybe the job would just be good because of the free pizza, but Clarissa did like cooking and trying new recipes on the weekend. A job at a pizza restaurant might help her figure out whether she'd like to pursue her passion with cooking or whether another one of her other interests would provide a better career fit.

Clarissa bit her lip. There was still so much to consider, but Violet had done it all before. Clarissa was glad that she had a friend she could talk to about job-related stuff. "What else do I need to think about?"

Clarissa was glad that she had a friend she could talk to about job-related stuff.

ASK THE
EXPERT

Think about all the available workplaces around you and figure out which ones you might like to work at—*before* you start sending applications and writing your résumé and cover letters. It's worth it in the long term to think about whether a job will be a good fit. Plus, think about how each job might help you in your future career. If you're thinking about becoming a veterinarian, you could work at a pet store or dog day care center.

You may not always have the luxury of waiting for the perfect job, and that's OK! You may need to help your household with bills, buy lunch, or make other necessary purchases. But thinking about which types of jobs might suit you best can help steer you in the right direction when starting your job search.

Starting a job search can seem scary, especially if you've never done it. But most people have been in your position, including your friends, teachers, parents, and other trusted adults. Many schools and libraries also have books or resources to help teens find jobs that fit their interests. Soon, you'll be well on your way to earning an income!

GET **HEALTHY**

- Start by looking at the jobs around you as you go through your week. Which can you picture yourself doing? Ask friends, parents, and neighbors for suggestions as well.

- Make a list of your interests, skills, and ideal work environment. Which jobs fit well with the characteristics of your ideal job?

- Think carefully about how many hours you can work per week and when. Employers will want someone who can work more than a few hours per week, but you need to balance your work schedule with school requirements.

- Look for jobs that help you learn skills or explore career options you'd like to pursue down the road.

THE LAST WORD FROM **REBECCA**

Getting your first job can feel like a chicken-and-egg problem. Employers want experience, but how do you get that experience if no one will hire you without it?

I found one of my first jobs in high school through a friend. She'd started waitressing at the local diner, so I thought I'd give it a try. I found out that waitressing wasn't really my thing. I got flustered when a lot of customers came in at the same time. That job taught me I didn't like working with hungry people waiting for food! But with a few months of experience at the diner, I was able to get a job at a retail store, which was a better fit for me. There are many types of jobs out there. It may take some digging, but you'll find one that's right for you. And if you find that your first job isn't a good fit, you can always find a new one.

CHAPTER TWO

FIRST DAY ON THE JOB

Change is hard, and starting a new job—especially your first new job—is a *big* change. What if your boss is tough? What if you can't handle one of your key responsibilities? What if the interviewer made a mistake by giving you the job and realizes his or her error on your first day? You thought the stress of the job search would disappear now that you have a job, but instead it just transforms into a new type of stress!

The good news is this anxiety will soon be over. In all likelihood, your interviewer didn't make a mistake. The company has hired many employees and knows the skills and qualities to look for in applicants. Managers have also had new employees before and know which responsibilities might cause them problems. You'll probably watch someone perform your new responsibilities before you do them yourself. After that, you'll likely have someone checking that you're doing everything correctly. Starting a job can be scary, but your coworkers and supervisors can help ease your fears. Lucia learned that on her first day of work.

LUCIA'S STORY

Lucia had been both looking forward to and dreading today for a week. She'd told her friends that she was 90 percent excited and 10 percent stressed about starting her new job, but it was really more like 50-50. She *needed* this job at the bagel shop. Money had been tight at home since her sister was born last spring. Lucia saw the creases in her dad's brow while he sat at the kitchen table paying bills. Lucia wanted to contribute some money to the house so things weren't so tight at the end of the month.

Lucia sat outside the bagel shop in her car for 20 minutes, nervously tapping on the steering wheel. She hadn't wanted to be late on her first day of work, but she'd left too early after school and had almost half an hour to spare. When she'd scrolled

through the last of her friends' social media updates, Lucia took
a deep breath and got out of her car. They wouldn't be too mad at
her for showing up ten minutes early, right?

The bell on the door of the shop seemed to tinkle a welcome
as she walked in, and the scent of fresh bagels felt like a hug.
Other than Lucia, there were only two employees at the shop.
Rachel, who had interviewed Lucia for the position, took orders
and helped customers. Her husband, Mark, worked in the
kitchen. It had been just the two of them, Rachel had said during
the interview, but the business was getting busier during the
weekend breakfast rush and after school, so they needed some
extra hands.

"Hey, Lucia! You're early," Rachel called from behind the counter.

"Hi!" Lucia said, plastering on a smile. "I figured if I came a few minutes early, I could watch you and learn what to do." And if she'd sat in the car any longer, Lucia would have bitten her fingernails down to nothing.

Rachel laughed. "No need to worry about learning stuff! Today I'll be training you for your first shift anyway. We can get you up to speed before the rush."

Rachel pulled something out from under the counter and held it up. "This is your uniform shirt. I think it's your size. You'll need to wear this shirt during each of your shifts."

The shirt matched the one Rachel was wearing, with a large illustration of a cartoon bagel smiling on the front and the company's name and address on the back. The shirt made Lucia feel like part of the team. "It looks perfect."

> "I figured if I came a few minutes early, I could watch you and learn what to do."

TALK ABOUT IT

= Which job responsibilities might be difficult? Do you think those are the first things your new supervisor will ask you to do?

= It's more likely you'll start with simpler job responsibilities on your first day. What might those be?

Mark, who was wearing his own matching shirt, peeked out from the kitchen. "Welcome, Lucia! We're glad to have you."

Rachel opened the swinging door in the counter, letting Lucia through from the customer side of the store to the employee side. The shop looked different from here. Instead of facing bins of plain bagels, onion bagels, and everything bagels, she faced

the door, waiting for the next customer to walk in. Lucia felt overwhelmed. Just standing on this side of the counter felt like a lot of responsibility. What if a customer asked Lucia a question and she didn't know the answer? What if too many people arrived at the same time and got upset about waiting their turn?

Lucia took a deep breath and tried to calm down. She pulled her uniform shirt over the top she was already wearing. If she didn't feel official, she could at least look official.

What if a customer asked Lucia a question and she didn't know the answer?

"The first thing you'll train on is the bagel slicer," Rachel said. "That may sound scary, but using the slicer is really easy. Go ahead and wash your hands and put on plastic gloves while I help this customer, and then we can get started."

Lucia glanced over her shoulder. There were two customers in line. She hadn't even noticed. After washing and drying, she held up clean, gloved hands. "Check."

Rachel slid a plain bagel into the slicer. The rectangular, silver slicer had a large blade down the middle. It reminded Lucia of the guillotines she'd learned about in history class. "All you have to do is load the bagel into the slicer and fit this piece on top,"

Rachel said. "Then you press down and voilà!" Rachel lifted the handle and showed Lucia the two bagel halves.

"That didn't seem so bad," Lucia said, looking at the bagel.

"Your turn!" Rachel said. She handed Lucia an everything bagel and pointed to the other bagel slicer.

Lucia fumbled a bit getting the bagel into the slicer with her gloved hands, but it really was as easy as Rachel said. She breathed a sigh of relief when she pressed down and the bagel sliced perfectly into two pieces. Some of Lucia's anxiety about her first day melted away. She could handle this!

"Condiments are to the left of the bagel case," Rachel said. She grabbed a knife from a tub of water and used it to spread butter onto half of the plain bagel. Lucia watched how much she used, making a mental note to copy that.

"We have every type of cream cheese you can imagine," Rachel added. "Plain, chive, strawberry, honey, you name it. But don't worry if you can't remember them all. There's a handy cheat sheet behind the register that lists the flavors of the day." Rachel's other bagel half got chive cream cheese. Lucia spread her practice bagel with

TALK ABOUT IT

= How would you handle learning new tasks on your first day? What are some things you could do that might make training easier?

= Why do you think Lucia felt so anxious on her first day?

= What would you tell a friend who is about to start a new job?

honey-flavored cream cheese. It looked delicious. Too bad Lucia couldn't eat it.

"We have other toppings like smoked salmon, peanut butter, and hazelnut spread. Mark will cook eggs in the kitchen if a customer orders that. Otherwise, the routine is pretty simple. You'll get the hang of it." Just as Rachel finished the demonstration, the bell on the door tinkled. Rachel smiled and said, "Your first customer."

"Otherwise, the routine is pretty simple. You'll get the hang of it."

Lucia turned to the customer, ready to fill her first order. "How can I help you?" she asked. She still felt nervous about getting things right, but Lucia was confident that Rachel would help her every step of the way.

ASK THE

EXPERT

The only way to get past first-day stress is to do what Lucia did: work with it. It's natural to be nervous about facing something new, but remember, your new supervisor wants you to succeed and feel confident in your job. Plus, your boss picked you from everyone who applied for the job for a reason!

Head to your first day with an open mind. Ask any questions you may have about the way things are done or how you'll be trained. Don't think your questions are stupid, and don't assume you ought to get everything right on the first try. If you're attentive, willing to learn, and persistent, after a few days of work you'll be comfortable with your new responsibilities and know your coworkers. In fact, you'll probably feel better and more confident after the first hour or two. A new job can take some getting used to. Expect some bumps in the road along the way. But if you find that after a few weeks you still don't feel like a good fit for the position, you may want to consider other options.

GET **HEALTHY**

- Think about your work environment before you show up for the first day. Will you be on your feet and need special shoes? Do you need any protective equipment? Do employees wear uniforms? These are questions to ask before your first day so you know how to prepare.

- Arrive early to your first shift. Give yourself plenty of time in case the weather is bad or it takes you a long time to find a parking spot.

- Clarify what you'll be doing on your first few shifts. Will you need to interact with customers and perform your job tasks? Or will you just be filling out forms and watching training videos? Knowing what to expect can help you feel more comfortable and ease any first-day anxiety.

THE LAST WORD FROM **REBECCA**

I would love to tell you all about my first day at my first job, but you know what? I can't even remember it. If it wasn't memorable, it couldn't have been all that bad!

Many first days are actually rather dull. They're full of things including filling out paperwork, listening to training presentations, and setting up computer usernames and passwords. You'll meet people including your supervisor, coworkers, and people who work in other departments. In fact, first days are often so full of preparation that there's not a lot of time left to actually work. There's a lot to take in on your first day, but you're on your way to learning new skills and earning money.

CHAPTER THREE

HOW TO FIND WORK

O nce you've thought of some jobs that interest you, how do you find a workplace to send an application to? Maybe you've decided you want to work at a pet store, but there are three pet stores nearby. Or maybe all you know is that you want to work with animals, but you're not sure whether there are options in addition to the pet stores. One strategy may be looking for resources that will help you think beyond obvious job options. Your local library will have career guides that list requirements for many jobs. Job-search websites publish research on trends in the employment market, including promising career paths. Additionally, your local chamber of commerce has lists of companies in your community.

Tell your family and friends that you're looking for a job! They may know of open positions. Your school may keep a list of jobs available in your community or provide access to college and career-preparation tools. It's worth investing some time in identifying the opportunities that best suit you. Rashida learned that when she started her job search.

RASHIDA'S STORY

Once Rashida started seriously considering getting a job, she suddenly saw jobs *everywhere*. Every place she went could be a potential workplace. It started to get overwhelming.

As she turned onto her street on her way home from soccer practice, she waved at her neighbor, Nabeeha. Nabeeha waved back with her free hand. Her other hand held three dog leashes. The dogs tugged her down the street at a brisk pace. Rashida's dad had shown her Nabeeha's dog-walking flyer last year when she'd started looking for clients. It seemed like Nabeeha's business was booming.

Rashida thought about the list of job openings that she'd picked up from her guidance counselor. It included positions such as checking in books at the library, leading summer camp classes at a city park, and stocking shelves at the grocery store.

It seemed like Nabeeha's business was booming.

Seeing Nabeeha outside on a sunny spring day made Rashida think back to the list she'd made when she first started looking for a job. She'd written down her interests, skills she'd like to use, and preferred working environments. When she got home, Rashida dug the list out of her bedside drawer. The first thing listed was her interest in working outdoors. Now that she thought about it, work wouldn't feel as demanding if she was outside rather than in a stuffy office or a crowded store.

TALK ABOUT IT

= Why might Rashida get a
list of jobs from the guidance
counselor? How could he help
her find a job?

= Why might a seasonal job work
better for some teens? Why
might others prefer a
part-time job?

The position at the city park might fit all of Rashida's needs. It didn't start until the summer, so Rashida couldn't earn any money for a few more months. However, in many ways Rashida thought a summer job might be the perfect fit. With the soccer season in full swing and the need to study for final exams once the season ended, there was no way she could start a new job yet. A camp counselor position would only last the summer, but it would give her something to put on her résumé to help her get a job in the fall if she wanted.

Rashida turned on her family's computer and went to the city parks website. She found a job description and list of qualifications for the job. But Rashida frowned when she saw that the application required a résumé. Rashida had never made a résumé before and didn't know what to include. She rubbed her face. What was she supposed to do?

***

The next morning, Rashida stopped by the guidance counselor's office before classes. She hadn't applied for the camp counselor job. She'd stared at a blank text document for almost an hour before giving up to work on her school assignments.

Mr. Kennedy was at his desk when Rashida knocked on his office door. "Hi Rashida!" he said. "How's the job search going?"

"Horrible," Rashida said as she slumped down into the empty chair. She handed him the paper he'd given her the day before, with the camp counselor job circled in yellow highlighter. "I have to submit a résumé for this job, but I've never *had* a job before. It's hopeless."

Mr. Kennedy hummed and turned back to his computer to type in the job website's address. "Résumés can feel challenging," he said, "but often you'd be surprised by what kind of experience you can include." He clicked around for a bit before turning back with a smile.

"It says here on the job page that one of the requirements is babysitting experience. Do you have any of that?"

Rashida was surprised. Sure, she babysat for the second grader down the street, but she hadn't thought it was a *real* job. Certainly not for a résumé. "Yeah, I watch a second grader down the street every Wednesday night while his mom works at the hospital," she said.

"Perfect!" Mr. Kennedy said. He smiled. "That's a great thing to put down for previous experience, especially since the website asked for it. You can also add any other languages you speak, computer programs you use, or just about anything else you have experience in."

Rashida breathed a sigh of relief. She spoke Arabic at home with her parents and brothers, and she'd built herself a basic website last summer when she wanted to show off some of her photography. She hadn't realized that those things could help her get a job.

During her lunch break, Rashida went to the library to finish her résumé and application. It was easier than she thought to fill an entire page with her education, skills, and experience. As she headed to her fourth-period class, she felt like she was on the way to her first job.

ASK THE

EXPERT

Many people find it daunting to write a résumé. It's easy to understand why. You're summarizing your experience, skills, and accomplishments all on one page. Sometimes you may feel like you have too much information to possibly fit on one page. Other times, you may struggle to find enough experience to make the page seem full.

Ask friends or older siblings whether you can look at their résumés to get ideas. Often, adding items such as languages, skills, academic interests, clubs, sports, community organizations, and leadership positions you've held can showcase your talents on a résumé if you don't have previous work experience. If you apply for jobs that are looking for your unique experience and skills, you're more likely to be successful. Don't forget to ask for feedback from trusted adults to help improve your résumé and make sure there aren't any spelling mistakes.

Once you have your first résumé, remember to look at it every couple of months and add new skills and experience. You may be surprised by how much you learn from your first job.

GET **HEALTHY**

- Getting a job is a big project. The best way to ensure that you don't feel overwhelmed is to break it down into smaller steps.

- Consult career guides available at your library or online. Check out the skills required for careers that interest you. Do you have those skills? Can you start developing them?

- Brainstorm as many potential employers and jobs as you can. Consult friends and family, job lists from your school's guidance office, and businesses you see around town.

- Do some research on the potential employers and jobs you've identified. Which ones match best with your preferences? Talk to people who can tell you more about these jobs.

- Apply to a few jobs each week so the work isn't overwhelming. Don't worry if the first job application is a bit intimidating. They'll get easier as you go.

THE LAST WORD FROM **REBECCA**

Applying for jobs is stressful, especially your first job, but don't let the stress of job hunting keep you from getting started. I've changed jobs several times in my life. My first job after college was working in finance in New York City. But now, I work as a freelancer. Being a freelancer means I'm always looking for new jobs. And I have to update my résumé a lot!

Over time, it's become easier to talk about my work experience and other skills on my résumé. Sometimes when I get overwhelmed, I look at old versions I've saved on my computer to see how far I've come. Once you make your first résumé, you'll be well on your way to sending out applications for jobs you truly love!

CHAPTER FOUR

MANAGING YOUR MONEY

Receiving your first paycheck feels like a milestone on the road to adulthood. You set out to get a job and make some money, and now you've done just that. Then you look at the amount on your check and see it's not quite as large as you thought it would be.

There are many reasons why your paycheck may be smaller than you thought. Your gross pay is your hourly pay rate multiplied by the number of hours you work. But there are many deductions from your gross pay. Employers deduct federal, state, and sometimes local income taxes from employee paychecks. These deductions include taxes that fund programs such as Social Security and Medicare. While it may sting to see these numbers disappear from your check each month, these deductions help you in the long run by funding health care and your own retirement.

When you decided to get a job, you may have come up with a long list of things you needed or wanted to buy. If your expenses are big—such as a car and car insurance, cell phone and service contract, or college—you'll need to save money over time to accumulate enough. It may be time to start thinking about a budget.

But even if you don't have a lot of large expenses, you may still need a budget to help keep track of your money. Iris found out the hard way that she needed a budget.

IRIS'S STORY

Iris was so excited to receive her first paycheck on Friday afternoon that she texted her best friend Beth before she left work.

Iris: First paycheck after filing tons of paperwork at the law office. Let's celebrate!

Beth: I'm in!

Iris: Be there in 10 minutes.

Iris picked Beth up at her house and together they drove to the mall. Their first stop was the bank, where Iris deposited her check. The teller explained to her how to endorse the check by signing the back. She typed some numbers into her computer

TALK ABOUT IT

= Do you have a bank account? Do you need one?

= How would you feel if you were in Iris's place with your first paycheck in hand?

= How would you feel if you were in Beth's place, with your best friend ready to celebrate a first paycheck?

and then handed Iris a slip of paper to show she'd added $180 to Iris's account balance. It was more money than Iris had ever had in her account all at once.

"Now we can celebrate my new job!" Iris said.

As the girls walked through the mall, Iris saw her favorite coffee shop, the one where Mom only occasionally bought her a drink. "A mocha would be the perfect beverage to celebrate," Iris said. "My treat." She felt very adult as she slid her debit card through the reader.

"Thanks!" Beth said. They sipped their warm, sweet beverages as they window shopped. Just as they finished their drinks, they arrived at their favorite fashion store. Luckily for them, the store was having a sale!

"Buy one item, get a second at half price," Beth said. "Now I wish I had a job!"

"Oh." Iris held up a silky silver blouse. "I'd look so professional in this." Iris had noticed the classic cuts of the clothes her boss wore. Iris had nothing like that in her closet except for a couple of dresses she wore when she went to church or dinners out with her family.

"Get it!" Beth encouraged her. "You can afford it. You know what they say, you should dress for success."

"It would go great with this." Iris pulled a pair of pleated black pants off the rack. "But that's a lot of money."

Beth smiled. "Well, it's buy one, get one 50 percent off."

"Right." Iris laughed. "I love having a job. I'll try them on."

The outfit looked amazing. Iris imagined her future self with a law degree plus the knowledge and confidence to advise clients like her boss did.

Beth and Iris followed shopping with dinner at the Mexican restaurant in the mall, then a romantic comedy they'd been dying to see at the movie theater. It was the most fun Friday night Iris could remember having. They did all of her favorite things.

"This was the best night ever," Beth said as they drove home later that night. Iris felt a warm glow inside. She'd done this. She'd found a job, made it through her first two weeks, and

> "I love having a job. I'll try them on."

TALK ABOUT IT

▪ What expenses or desired purchases inspired you to get your first job? How can you make sure your paycheck goes toward those purchases?

▪ If you hope to buy something large, such as a car, how can you save money from several paychecks to accumulate enough money?

received her first paycheck. She and Beth could do this again any time. It made her feel like her future was bright and her days of asking Mom for money were over.

Then, a ding came from the car's dashboard. The gas tank icon lit up. "Darn, I need to stop for gas," Iris said.

"Good thing you got paid," Beth said.

Iris agreed, but it seemed odd. Hadn't she just put gas in the car last week? Then she remembered she was driving more than usual. She'd worked three days each week. She'd need to remember to set aside money for gas. Iris slid her card into the payment slot at the pump and made another unpleasant discovery.

"Approved: $22.50 maximum charge," the screen said.

Iris knew it would take $30 to fill up her tank. Why was she only approved for $22.50 when she'd just been paid? She pulled up her bank's app on her phone:

Pipin' Hot Java: $12.50

City Outfitters: $60

Puerto Vallarta Mexican Restaurant: $40

Summerset Cinema: $45.

Iris did some quick math. She'd spent $157.50 tonight! She only had $22.50 left, and that was about to go into her gas

Why was she only approved for $22.50 when she'd just been paid?

TALK ABOUT IT

- Have you ever spent money on something and then regretted the purchase later?

- How do you think Iris felt when she realized there was only $22.50 left in her account?

- What do you think Iris might do differently when she gets her next paycheck?

49

tank. She'd meant to celebrate, but she hadn't meant to celebrate *that much.*

Iris decided she could get by on half a tank of gas, which would leave her with a few dollars until she got paid again in a couple weeks. She tried to keep her enthusiasm up for the rest of the drive home with Beth. But when she got home and her mom asked how her celebration was, she couldn't hide her disappointment any longer.

"I'm broke!" She dropped her bag from the clothes store onto the living room table and flopped down on the couch.

Her mom pulled out the blouse and slacks. "These look like they'll be perfect for your new job, but maybe you need a budget to manage the money you're making now."

"A budget?" That seemed like some serious adulting, but Iris didn't want to feel broke just a few hours after getting paid again. "How do I do that?"

"Creating a budget isn't hard," her mom said. "You can even make a simple budget in a spare notebook for now. It just requires listing the things you want or need to spend money on and comparing that to the amount of money you've earned

> Iris didn't want to feel broke just a few hours after getting paid again.

to make sure your expenses aren't bigger than your paycheck. You took the job to save for college and a new cell phone right?"

Iris nodded. "I wanted some money to spend going out with friends too, but now I don't have anything left for the things I wanted to save for."

"You could return your new outfit," her mom suggested. When she saw Iris's frown, she added, "Or you could call that an investment in your new job and set aside a certain amount of money from future paychecks for each of your goals before you start spending. Opening a savings account for that money might help, because then you wouldn't be able to spend it with your debit card. These are all good things to put in your new budget."

"That sounds good since I now know how easy it is to spend more than I mean to with a debit card," Iris said. "Tomorrow I'll open a savings account, and next weekend Beth and I will be back to free movies on this couch."

> "I now know how easy it is to spend more than I mean to with a debit card."

ASK THE

EXPERT

You expected earning a paycheck to give you financial freedom, but creating a budget can feel like the opposite. It limits the amount you can spend on certain things. On the other hand, ending up in Iris's situation with your newly earned money slipping through your fingers can be frustrating. You took your new job for a reason. You might have bills to pay or something you want to save up to buy. A budget is a tool to make sure that your money goes where you want it and your bills are covered before you spend money on fun stuff.

Iris might be perfectly satisfied with having splurged on a new-job celebration, but she wants to spend her second paycheck more carefully. She took her job to save for college, pay for gas, buy a cell phone, and have money to go out with friends. Now, she's realized she also wants a more grown-up look for her wardrobe.

Everyone's budget looks different. Yours might have these expenses: gas, cell phone savings, college savings, and fun money. By limiting fun money, you may not be able to pay for coffee, new clothes, and a movie every week. But it does mean you can save money for things that are important to you. Budgeting is all about trade-offs, and it's a great skill to learn once you start earning an income.

GET **HEALTHY**

- Look at your paycheck. How much money do you have in hand? Spend that money, not money you haven't yet earned.

- Think about your expenses. Which things are your responsibility? Your list may include clothes, lunch money, household bills, car insurance, gas, and going out with friends.

- If you'd like to save for a car, college, or some other high-cost items, open a savings account. Setting aside money from each paycheck will help you reach your goals over time.

- Compare your cash to your expenses and saving goals. Do you have more than you need to fund expenses plus the amount you want to save? If not, what expenses have you listed that aren't must-haves?

- What will you do if an unexpected expense comes up? It's a good idea to set aside some money for unexpected expenses so that these events don't leave you scrambling.

THE LAST WORD FROM **REBECCA**

Learning to manage money is tough. Like Iris, you might spend your first paycheck a lot faster than you'd like. Don't feel bad if you don't make the best decisions the first time you have some money to spend. Many people learn how to manage money by doing it badly and deciding they want to do better.

When I was working at my first job in New York City, I wasn't making a lot of money. And New York City is an expensive place to live! Boy, did I need a budget. I stretched my money, and you can too. It just takes some time and patience to figure out what works for you.

CHAPTER FIVE

MANAGING YOUR TIME

Managing your time can be tricky even without a job. It may be hard to juggle homework, family commitments, time with friends, and other things in your schedule. So what do you do when you also have a job that takes up ten to 15 hours per week?

That may not sound like a lot of time, and it may amount to only working two shifts during the school week with another shift on the weekend. However, think about how much free time you have in your schedule right now. You can't call in to work because you have an English paper due the next day, but you also can't skip your English paper because you have to work! It's easy for tasks to pile up when you're running from one place to the next.

Crunch times like that can be really stressful. After getting a job, it may seem like you don't have any time to just be yourself anymore. Margot certainly felt that way when her dog-walking business took off.

MARGOT'S STORY

Margot sat down under a tree in the shade while she let the two dogs she was walking, Pepper and Marshmallow, drink from a doggy water fountain nearby. She took her job as a dog walker seriously and liked to be present for her furry clients as they got their exercise and fresh air, but today was different. Today, Margot had received her first C- on an Algebra 2 test. Actually, her first C- on *any* test since entering high school.

She sighed and rested her forehead on her knees. Her parents were going to be so mad. When she started her dog-walking business last year, she'd promised that it wouldn't affect her grades. She knew when they saw her Algebra 2 grade, they'd surely make her quit walking dogs. Then how would she save for college? But if she kept getting poor grades on tests, she might not even get into college!

Pepper, a little black Scottish terrier, started yapping and pulling on his leash, wanting to continue their walk. Marshmallow was quieter, but she slobbered water everywhere, as bulldogs

TALK ABOUT IT

= Have you ever run out of time to study for a test or write a paper? How did it make you feel?

= How many hours a week do you think you could work without your grades slipping?

= Which activities in your schedule would you be willing to give up to take a job?

typically did. She tugged at the leash as well, which made Margot finally glance up to see what was wrong. Marcus, her eight-year-old neighbor, was whizzing down the sidewalk on his bike. He wasn't looking where he was going, and he was headed right for Pepper!

"Move over, guys!" Margot gave the dogs an urgent tug onto the grass. She called "Share the sidewalk" to Marcus as he flew past and then shoved her phone in her pocket where it belonged. Staring at that grade wasn't going to change it, and it might get one of the dogs hurt.

Pepper had been her first client. When she first started walking him, she'd had no problem finishing homework and studying for tests. Margot had always relaxed for her first hour after school before starting her homework. So instead, she used that hour to walk Pepper. Marshmallow was easy too. Since she could walk them both together, adding a second dog only added a few minutes to her schedule. But after Margot had put flyers around the neighborhood, she'd found three more clients. That meant Margot had to spend two hours between school and

homework walking dogs since she couldn't safely handle five dogs at once.

The extra hour each day had been a little stressful at first, but after a few weeks Margot got used to the tighter schedule. But this week, on top of her regular duties, Margot was house-sitting and feeding the cats for one of her customers while they were on vacation. When Mrs. Chen had asked, it hadn't seemed like that much extra work. However, Margot found it really hard to fit in the time between walking dogs, school, and everything else in her schedule. She hadn't been able to study for the math test, and there was another one coming up next Monday before the Chens returned from vacation. Margot couldn't let the cats go hungry or the dogs go unwalked, but she also couldn't neglect her schoolwork.

> Margot had always relaxed for her first hour after school before starting her homework. So instead, she used that hour to walk Pepper.

TALK ABOUT IT

▪ **What are your priorities? Your grades? Making money? Work experience and getting recommendations?**

▪ **Where do family and friends fit into your new, busy schedule?**

Marshmallow stopped by a tree to do her business, and Pepper tried to eat some blades of grass while they waited. Margot bent down to scoop the poop, and when she stood back up, Marshmallow was staring at her, tail wagging.

"What am I going to do, girl?" Margot asked Marshmallow. Marshmallow just stared at her. She didn't have any good answers either.

***

When Margot finally got home from the Chens' house, the sun was starting to set and her mom was trying to get the family order for pizza night. But Margot wasn't hungry. Her stomach was upset from trying to figure out what to do.

Margot had a social studies paper due tomorrow. She'd written an outline and read her sources, but she knew she'd be up late writing it. She had a world history test on Friday, so if she didn't get enough sleep tonight, there'd be no way to catch up until the weekend. Plus, she'd need to see whether she could make the corrections on that Algebra 2 test for partial credit. There might be time tomorrow morning during her free

TALK ABOUT IT

= Would you to able to say no to extra work if you knew you couldn't handle it? Or would you say yes and hope for the best?

= How might big tests or projects make it more difficult to have a job during school?

= What could you do ahead of time to make everything work out?

period if she got to school early enough. Even though there wasn't much that Margot could do to fix her busy schedule that week, she resolved to never overbook herself like this again. Ten hours a week walking dogs was all that she could handle while still maintaining her good grades. Even though other projects or jobs might not seem like a lot of work at the time, Margot knew that she needed to better manage her time if she wanted to accomplish all of her goals.

ASK THE

EXPERT

Adding a new job to your schedule can make you feel like there aren't enough hours in the day. Studies show that working too many hours during the school year can harm a student's grades and participation in other activities. If the new job is important, take a careful look at how you spend your time now and consider which activities you could cut to free up hours for work. For example, if you need to have a job, you may need to work on time management to fit in all of your responsibilities every day. Know your priorities and be true to them when you need to make trade-offs. Leave time for family, friends, and relaxation.

For many people, a regular routine is a great way to feel confident that there's time for everything. Ask for regular work hours so you know when you'll be free for homework and other activities. Make sure you're disciplined about doing homework and other responsibilities on your days off. This kind of discipline is difficult to stick to, but being ahead is so much better than being late and losing sleep.

Learning how to juggle more responsibilities is one challenge of having a job while also being a student. However, if you keep on top of your daily and weekly schedule, you'll be able to succeed at both. Whatever your future plans are, good grades will help.

GET **HEALTHY**

- Block out your last week on a blank calendar or piece of paper—the time you spent at school, playing sports, working at your job, doing homework, taking care of other responsibilities, spending time with friends and family, and sleeping. Is the calendar what you expected?

- Think about what's making your schedule feel hectic. Are you short on time for homework, sleep, hanging out with friends, or just relaxing? How many hours do you need to free up to make your schedule work?

- You won't be happy or productive if you're working every minute. Make sure you schedule regular times for breaks.

- If your schedule is tight, consider ways you can use your time more efficiently. Are there still not enough hours in the day? Maybe you can study at your job when business is slow, or have study parties with friends instead of watching movies.

THE LAST WORD FROM **REBECCA**

When you recorded where you spent your time, did you notice you spend more hours than you thought on activities that aren't actually that important to you? You might have free chunks of time before school or between school and work that you spend on your phone or in other low-priority activities. If you want to start working, you may need to use that time more productively.

When I first started pursuing writing as a career, I didn't have much free time. I squeezed writing into any gap I could find, including while I was waiting for my kids at soccer practice. It's not always easy, but if your new job is important to you, you can find the time for it.

CHAPTER SIX

JOB INTERVIEWS

Once you've filled out a few job applications, the worst part of the process starts—waiting. Some businesses may take weeks or even months to decide on the person they want to hire. That waiting can be frustrating. It's hard to be patient about a decision that's so important for you. What's taking so long? Does this mean the manager just took your application, crumpled it up, and tossed it into the trash?

Just when you've given up hope on the jobs you applied for, the phone may ring or you might get an email. The manager of the company you were so interested in a couple of weeks ago wants to set up time to talk! Now you go from frustration to panic. You have a job interview! What should you wear? What will they ask? What if you say the wrong thing? Sofía had these worries when she got a call from her favorite store about an interview.

SOFÍA'S STORY

Sofía was at the library doing homework with her friend Jules when her phone started ringing. Mrs. Yu, the librarian sitting at the desk, lifted an eyebrow. "Sorry," Sofía mumbled as she jammed her thumb on the volume button. OK, she should have silenced her phone, but who calls instead of texting?

"Aren't you going to answer that?" Jules asked, nodding toward Sofía's phone.

It was an unknown phone number in her area. "It's probably a wrong number."

"Or it could be someone calling about a job." Jules raised her eyebrows. "You've been waiting to hear back from those places for like two weeks!"

The first few days, Sofía had jumped every time her phone pinged with a notification, but as day after day passed, she'd lost hope. "Do you think?" Sofía asked, excited.

Her phone pinged again. She had a voice mail. Sofía could barely contain her joy. Wrong numbers didn't usually leave voice mails. She grabbed her phone and jogged to the library lobby, where she could have

TALK ABOUT IT

▪ How would you feel if you were waiting to hear back from companies about positions you applied for? Would you feel excited or nervous?

▪ Why do you think people apply for multiple jobs at the same time? What is the benefit to doing that?

> ## Sofía jotted down the name and phone number with trembling fingers.

a quick conversation without making the librarian upset. The message was from her favorite clothing store at the mall!

Sofía jotted down the name and phone number with trembling fingers. Then, after reminding herself that everyone said she had a great eye for fashion—she needed a quick confidence boost—she called the number.

"Utopia, fun fashions for teens. How can I help you?" said the person who answered.

"Hi, this is Sofía. I just missed a call from Maggie. Is she available?" Sofía's heart was beating fast.

"Thanks for calling me back so quickly," Maggie said. "I liked your answers on the job application and was wondering if you could stop by the store on Saturday morning so we could talk."

"Yes, I'd love to," Sofía gushed. Utopia was her first-choice job. She was already thinking about how awesome her wardrobe would be with an employee discount at the store.

"Wonderful!" Maggie said. "Does 10:00 a.m. work?"

"Yes, that's fine." She could talk to her parents about getting a ride tonight.

"Great, I look forward to meeting you." Maggie ended the call.

Sofía rushed back to share the great news with Jules. Jules practically shrieked, and Mrs. Yu cleared her throat. But nothing could dampen Sofía's spirits right now. She was so close to a job with Utopia. How could she wait two days for the interview? Then Jules's next question brought her back down to Earth.

"What do you think she'll ask you in the interview?"

"What do you think she'll ask you in the interview?"

"Oh." Sofía hadn't thought about that. "This is my first actual interview. I have no idea!"

"Lucky you have a friend who's already interviewed for a job and gotten it," Jules said. "Pretend I'm the manager at Utopia."

Sofía felt nervous at the thought of answering interview questions, even from Jules, but she knew this would be a good way to prepare for the real thing. "OK, shoot."

Jules sat up straight in the library chair and put on a serious

TALK ABOUT IT

= What questions do you think you could be asked in a job interview?

= Put yourself in the position of the manager. What would you want to know about a new employee?

= What questions do you want to ask the manager about the company and the position?

interview face. "Tell me why you want this job at Utopia fashions."

Jules's good posture made Sofía sit up straighter too, but she still wasn't sure about how to answer the question. "Uh, because I need to make some money. Isn't that kind of obvious?"

Jules cracked up, breaking her serious interviewer demeanor. "Do you think she might like you better if you said you love the store's clothes and that you stop by and check out their clothes every time you're in the mall?"

Sofía smacked her forehead with her palm. "Of course! I do stop by all the time. And that answer would make it seem like I could help the store's customers with fashion advice."

"Exactly." Jules got her interviewer face back on. "What hours would you be available to work?"

TALK ABOUT IT

= Being prepared for your interview will help you project confidence. What else makes you feel confident?

= Could you ask a friend or family member to help you with a practice interview? Who would be a good fit to help you? What advice could they give you?

"That answer would make it seem like I could help the store's customers with fashion advice."

73

That was another good question. Sofía took a second to think about this answer more carefully. When she stumbled, Jules offered more tips and talked about what happened during her interview at the frozen yogurt shop.

After a few more questions, Jules pronounced Sofía ready for her interview. "Plan to get there 15 minutes early. That way if it's one of those days when there are no parking spots at the mall, you won't be late for your interview. And wear something that looks professional, like a skirt or slacks. That way the interviewer can tell you're serious about the job."

"What would I do without you?" Sofía said with a laugh as she and Jules left the library. She was so glad she'd been studying with Jules when she'd received that call.

> After a few more questions, Jules pronounced Sofía ready for her interview.

ASK THE

EXPERT

You should be prepared to answer several common interview questions before any interview. *Why do you want to work for this company? What skills do you have that will help you succeed in this position? What are your longer-term career interests?* These questions aren't difficult, but you'd be surprised how many job candidates come to interviews unprepared. Don't let that be you!

You've already researched the company and position, but now that you're going to talk to a manager in person, you'll want to dig deeper. Finding out all you can about the company will set you apart from other candidates and show that you're genuinely interested in the job. It will also raise some questions you can ask during your interview. An interview is a two-way street. Think of it like you're interviewing the company right back! Ask about the company's business, responsibilities that come with the position, and which types of employees are successful in this position. Companies like to hire people who are interested in their business, not just any job. You want to make sure that you're going to be a good fit.

GET **HEALTHY**

- Preparation is the best way to ensure your interview will be successful. Think about what questions your interviewer is likely to ask and have answers prepared in advance.

- Research the company you're interviewing with and show genuine interest in it. Companies want employees who are enthusiastic about their work.

- No one lands every job they apply for. Apply for a few different positions. That way, if some of the companies are looking for skills you don't have, you still have some options.

- If you aren't hired after the interview, remember that your first job search is a learning experience. Give yourself some time and flexibility to find the right thing for you. Keep on applying for positions until you get a yes!

THE LAST WORD FROM **REBECCA**

Interviewing, waiting to hear back from potential employers, and rejections are the hard part of the job-search process. I wish there was a way to make this easier, but it's a challenge we all face at one time or another. Just remember, you only need one person to say yes!

When I was in college, my friends and I posted our job-search rejections on the wall outside our dorm rooms. The letters reminded each of us that we weren't the only ones facing rejection. We were all searching for our dream jobs, and each rejection was a step on our journey. Before the end of the school year, we'd all received invitations for interviews, passed them, and received job offers. We were on our way to earning an income!

CHAPTER SEVEN

QUITTING YOUR JOB

Getting your first job isn't the end of your career trajectory—it's only the beginning. After you've held your first job for a few months, you'll want to take stock of whether it still meets your original goals. Are you continuing to learn new skills? Earning enough money for your expenses? Or do you think you might want to take what you've learned and move to a job that better suits your interests and career goals?

No one can answer these questions for you. A job is work, and not every part of it is going to be fun. You need to balance the pros and cons to decide whether you should stay or look for your dream job. Think carefully about what a new job looks like—perhaps it features more money, more hours, or responsibilities that fit better with your interests, skills, and ideal work environment.

If you identify a job that you think you'd enjoy more, learn more about it. Research the employer or see whether you can talk to someone who works for the company. What is the job really like? What are their favorite parts of the job, and what do they like the least? Now that you have a job, it's best not to let it go until you have a new one. Let's see how Allison wrestled with these issues.

ALLISON'S STORY

Allison hefted the gray plastic tub of dirty dishes from the clearing station and headed toward the kitchen. Her back ached from lugging heavy dishes around all afternoon and carrying a heavy backpack around at school. She'd dreamed of money for clothes that didn't come from the secondhand store when she took this job busing for the diner. She hadn't dreamed of building up her biceps.

Allison wiped sweat from her forehead after she set the tub on the counter by the dishwashing station. The kitchen was hot and steamy. The cooks joked with each other as they flipped burgers on the grill and assembled sandwiches.

Their job seemed fun, but Allison hated the heat. As she walked back to the clearing station with an empty bin to replace the

TALK ABOUT IT

= What do you like about your job? What do you not like about your job? Be thoughtful—remember, no job is perfect.

= Are you continuing to learn new things from your job or are you feeling stuck?

= What would a better job look like? Do you want a more challenging job? Better pay?

one she'd just removed, she thought about the servers' jobs. They didn't spend much time in the kitchen, but they needed to deal with customers. Allison knew customers were sometimes easy and sometimes tough, but the tips made it worth it, or so it seemed to her. She made minimum wage, while the waitresses made a base rate plus 15 to 20 percent of customer bills.

Allison had been in too much of a rush to get a job and too inexperienced to feel confident that she could get a better one. She wondered whether she could now.

Allison lifted the full tub from another clearing station. She was heading toward the kitchen when she noticed the manager was sitting at the desk in her office. It was time to ask for a promotion. Allison deposited the heavy tub full of dirty dishes in the kitchen and wiped her hands on her white apron. Her gut twisted with nerves as she walked to the manager's door.

> Allison had been in too much of a rush to get a job and too inexperienced to feel confident that she could get a better one. She wondered whether she could now.

"Hey, Sonia. I wanted to talk to you about transitioning to a server position. My time busing dishes has helped me to learn how the diner works, and I've watched how the servers manage customers and their food orders. I think I could do the job."

Sonia smiled, but Allison could tell it wasn't a "yes" smile. Her heart sank. "You're a hard worker and reliable, Allison, and we

like to promote from within. I'd definitely consider you for the next open position, but right now we have enough servers. In fact, some aren't getting as many hours as they'd like."

Allison's face flushed. "Oh, thanks." She turned to bus the next clearing station, feeling dejected.

TALK ABOUT IT

= What jobs do you see around you that you might like better?

= What companies might be a better fit?

= Have your interests, the skills you want to use on the job, and your ideal work environment changed based on your first job experience?

Later that night, Allison thought about what Sonia had said. She'd called Allison hardworking and reliable. She hadn't said Allison would be a bad server—just that there wasn't an open position at the diner. But there were plenty of other restaurants in town. In fact, the parking lot of the new noodles place always looked packed. Allison decided to stop by tomorrow and see whether they were hiring servers.

It turned out they were. The manager told Allison about the noodle restaurant's menu and her expectations for people waiting tables. She was glad that

Allison decided to stop by tomorrow and see whether they were hiring servers.

85

Allison already had experience working in a restaurant, even if Allison hadn't been a server before.

At the end of the conversation, she asked, "How soon can you start?" And just like that, Allison had a new job. When she got back to her car, she did a little happy dance. She'd done it! And she'd get paid more for her new job too. But then her happy dance slowed down when she realized that she'd have to quit her old job. Allison frowned. She liked Sonia and her coworkers at the diner. It was going to be hard to quit.

Allison decided to do it right away so she could get it over with. She took a deep breath and drove across town to the diner, where the evening shift was just getting started.

> And just like that, Allison had a new job.

TALK ABOUT IT

= How do you want people at your old job to remember you after you leave?

= Will you want a reference for your next job or in the future?

= What could you do to leave the job on a good note without hard feelings?

"Allison," Sonia said, surprised. "I didn't think you were on the schedule today."

"I'm not," Allison said. She nervously twisted the hem of her shirt. "Actually, I came by to put in my two weeks' notice. I've found another job." Allison grimaced at her own words.

Even though she knew changing jobs was the best thing for her future, it was still hard to leave her first job.

Allison was expecting the worst, so she was shocked when Sonia smiled and nodded. "I'm sad that you're leaving us, but happy that you found a job you wanted," Sonia said. "If a serving position opens here, I'll be sure to let you know. We'd love to have you back."

Allison smiled and thanked Sonia. While she expected to like working at the new restaurant, having an offer to come back here if it didn't work out was great to have in her back pocket. When she left the diner, she breathed a sigh of relief. It had been difficult to quit, but Allison knew she'd made the right decision.

ASK THE

EXPERT

Moving on to a new job is part of moving up the career ladder, learning new skills, and taking on greater responsibility. Just make sure you're looking at the pros and cons of both your current job and the new job you're considering with open eyes. Talk to people working at the company you'd like to join or at least in the same type of job to find out what it's really like. Make sure it will help move you toward your dream job by aligning with your interests, the skills you want to use and develop, and your ideal work environment.

Your new supervisor may want to contact employment references, or you may want your current supervisor to write a college reference for you. It's best to resign on a good note rather than leave your supervisor scrambling to get the work done without you. Your new employer will understand the need to give two weeks' notice because they would want the same courtesy. If you know someone who is looking for a job and might be a good fit, suggest that person apply to your old employer. Helping fill the position you're leaving is a great way to leave on good terms.

GET **HEALTHY**

- Make a list of all the things you've learned at your job. Think not only about skills but also the real-world knowledge you've gained about how companies work, as well as managing your time as you juggle school, work, and other responsibilities. Is there anything you can add to your résumé?

- Assess the pros and cons of leaving your current job. What aspects of the job will you miss after you leave? What aspects of the new job aren't aligned with your interests, skills, and ideal work environment?

- Take your time. It's fine to be ambitious, but you have a job. As long as you're comfortable in the position, there's no reason to let it go until you've found an even better job and been hired.

THE LAST WORD FROM **REBECCA**

I always find jobs difficult to leave. When you have a job, you know what's expected of you, you've become good at it, and you've made friends with your coworkers. It's difficult to leave all that behind for the unknown. It was particularly difficult when I was considering leaving my first position after college. I was working for an organization that I knew would look good on my résumé, but it was very slow to advance people to positions of more responsibility. I felt that if I stayed, I wouldn't continue to learn as much as I had in my first couple of years.

I landed a job that paid me more and invested in my training. I also found that I liked my new coworkers very much. In the end, we have to do what's right for our own careers. Sometimes that means staying at a company and waiting for a promotion, but when it means moving on, don't be afraid to do so.

CHAPTER EIGHT

HARASSMENT AT WORK

anding your first job and getting used to the work responsibilities is difficult. It's tremendously more difficult if you have an unfriendly workplace environment. For example, if you work with someone who doesn't seem to like you and avoids communicating with you, you'll likely have trouble completing tasks that require input from both of you.

Sometimes the workplace behavior of a boss, coworker, or customer can cross from unfriendly to illegal. This behavior may be a type of harassment motivated by race, gender, sexual orientation, or disability. A coworker may make an offensive comment about your skin color or hair, or someone may touch your body or property without your consent.

Sexual harassment is unwelcome behavior in the work environment that is initiated based on an employee's gender. It may include inappropriate jokes, verbal abuse, unwanted physical contact, or assault. Sexual harassment can create a hostile or offensive work environment or result in the victim being demoted, receiving a reduction in pay, or being fired.

Most companies have sexual harassment policies in place so that employees know which types of conduct are not appropriate and how to report a problematic behavior. Companies have every incentive to make sure their workplaces are friendly to employees, but this doesn't mean that everyone follows the guidelines in the company's policy. Lindsay found this out the hard way.

LINDSAY'S STORY

Lindsay loved her job at the coffee shop. She knew the regular customers by name and had their caffeinated drinks of choice served up for them by the time the cashier handed them their receipt. The money in the tip jar showed that the customers appreciated the prompt service and the care put into making the drinks. That was good, because money was tight at home now that her mom's hours had been cut back.

When Harper, her supervisor, pulled Lindsay aside to ask whether she'd want to work more hours, Lindsay jumped at the opportunity. "Nic just quit the six-to-nine p.m. shift," Harper told her. "She's not even coming in tonight."

"I'd love more hours." Lindsay mentally ticked through her homework assignments. "In fact, I can even start tonight. I'm ahead in most of my classes."

"That's great! The hours are yours. You'll be working with Ben. I'll introduce you when he arrives."

Harper looked like she wanted to hug her. "That's great! The hours are yours. You'll be working with Ben. I'll introduce you when he arrives."

Ben had worked at the coffee shop for six months, but Lindsay had never really met him. His shifts at night always started right when she was leaving for the day. The only thing Lindsay knew about Ben was that he was a lacrosse player at the local college, and she knew that only because sometimes his teammates would come in to hang out during his shifts. They'd arrive just as Lindsay would be in the middle of cleaning her station. The group was rowdy and hard to miss.

Lindsay's shift flew by with multiple complicated seasonal drink orders. Everyone wanted pumpkin spice lattes now that the leaves on the trees were turning. Harper told Lindsay to take her 30-minute lunch break just before six so she'd have some coverage before Harper left for the day. When Lindsay returned, more caffeinated and with one of the shop's tasty sandwiches in her belly, Harper introduced her to Ben.

"It's nice to meet you," Ben said with a dazzling smile. He shook Lindsay's hand, then gestured over his shoulder at two guys sitting near the window. They were flicking straw wrappers at each other. "David and Edgar are my friends from school, and they'll be providing the evening's entertainment."

Realizing they were being talked about, the guys waved back and smiled broadly.

Edgar gave her a hearty, "Welcome to the team," as if he was actually an employee at the shop. It made Lindsay laugh. But David's eyes slid up and down Lindsay's body in a way that made her really uncomfortable.

"*Hello*," David said, the word drawn out by more syllables than it required. Lindsay frowned. David might be just hanging out, but Lindsay was working. And she wasn't looking for that kind of attention anyway. However, neither Harper nor the other guys seemed to notice, so Lindsay let it go.

TALK ABOUT IT

▪ **Have you ever received unwanted attention from someone? What did you do? How would things be different if it happened at work?**

▪ **Why might Lindsay be uncomfortable talking to David about the situation? What about Ben?**

David's eyes slid up and down Lindsay's body in a way that made her really uncomfortable.

***

Harper left the shop at seven, when the after-work rush died down. Now it was just Lindsay and Ben until closing. The workload didn't seem like it would be a problem. The shop was pretty empty other than a few people studying and working on their laptops. However, Lindsay kept having to deal with David asking her questions that made her increasingly uncomfortable. Even when he was chatting with Edgar, he'd keep glancing her way while she worked. And when he wasn't busy, he'd come over and pepper her with questions and strange comments:

"What happened to Nic?"

"Will she be back in the shop tomorrow?"

"I don't mind that you've taken over for her. You're an upgrade."

The more uncomfortable Lindsay felt about David's attention, the more she

> Lindsay kept having to deal with David asking her questions that made her increasingly uncomfortable.

TALK ABOUT IT

= What would you do if you were in Lindsay's situation? Would you talk to David directly? Why or why not?

= If you didn't feel comfortable addressing either of the boys, whom could you ask for help?

wondered whether David might have had something to do with
Nic's quick departure. But Lindsay didn't have the option of
quitting her job while her family was having money trouble. She
gave David one-word answers to his questions and busied herself
cleaning tables and the coffee equipment, but all the while, she
wondered whether she'd have to put up with this every time she
worked past six. She knew she needed to change the situation,
but she wasn't sure how to do that.

Lindsay was so glad when nine o'clock finally arrived. She
faked a smile and wished them all good night as she grabbed her
bag. David stood up and said, "I'll walk you to your car."

"No thanks," Lindsay said. She headed quickly to the door before David could get up from his chair. Lindsay was thankful that she parked close to the door when she'd arrived earlier that afternoon. That way she could get into her car and take a deep breath to calm her nerves before she drove home.

The next day, Lindsay arrived early for her shift and asked Harper whether they could talk in the office for a moment. After Harper heard what had happened the night before, she said, "I'm so sorry. You shouldn't have had to deal with that. I'll speak to Ben tonight and David too if he's here. I never want you to feel unsafe at work."

Lindsay was so glad she had spoken up before things got worse. Harper had looked stunned, so Lindsay hoped that things would change for the better. "Thank you," Lindsay said. "I didn't know what to do."

"I'm glad you told me about the problem before it got any worse," Harper said. "And please let me know if anything else happens. That behavior is unacceptable."

Lindsay smiled. It made her feel better that her manager was on her side about David's behavior—or any other problems that might arise during her shifts.

"I'm glad you told me about the problem before it got any worse," Harper said.

ASK THE EXPERT

The most important thing to do when you are receiving unwanted advances at work or sexual harassment of any type is to address the issue directly. You can talk to the harasser if you feel comfortable doing so or talk to your supervisor.

If you talk to the harasser, tell them that their words or actions make you uncomfortable and that you want them to stop. If the behavior doesn't stop, you should put your concerns in writing. Document exactly what is happening at work that makes you feel uncomfortable.

If the problematic behavior doesn't stop, ask to see your company's sexual harassment policy and speak to your company's human resources department if it has one. If your employer doesn't take action to fix the situation, other avenues are open to you. These include filing a complaint with a government agency or suing the employer. However, filing a complaint with a government agency is a lengthy undertaking, and suing your employer can be both expensive and time consuming. The simplest course of action is having your employer correct the situation.

Most importantly, protect yourself. If you feel that the situation could escalate into violence, get immediate assistance.

GET HEALTHY

- You deserve to work in an environment that's free from harassment. If someone is making you uncomfortable at work, you should feel free to tell them to stop.

- Think about what you would do if someone were harassing you at work. Practice what you might say. Think about ways you could alert your manager to the problem.

- Make sure that you are safe. If you are worried that you won't be safe while your employer investigates your complaint, seek further assistance from someone who can help you.

THE LAST WORD FROM REBECCA

I had an incident that made me very uncomfortable at one of my early jobs after college. I was working with an out-of-state client who planned an after-work activity that I thought was incredibly inappropriate. I felt extremely uncomfortable and left immediately. I felt disrespected by the people who'd planned this activity and disappointed that coworkers had not stood up for me. After I reported the incident, the company did all the right things to fix the situation. If you do find yourself in a situation where you feel uncomfortable, I hope your employer gives you all the support that you deserve to remedy it.

Sexual harassment isn't the only form of harassment that can take place in the workplace. You shouldn't have to put up with racial harassment or bullying either. If you're the victim of any type of harassment, talk to your harasser if you feel comfortable doing so or report the incident to your supervisor for assistance.

A SECOND
LOOK

As you take your first steps into the working world, keep a couple of thoughts in mind. Your job search should always start with a review of your interests, the skills you want to use and develop, and the type of work environment you want. Many types of jobs are available in the world. You'll be happiest, though, if you find one that you enjoy and that helps you learn new skills.

The perfect job for you might not be the first one you see when you walk out your door, but it's worth investing time in research and networking to find it. You'll work many hours at any job, so finding a position you love and feel you're getting more than just a paycheck from is important. Sometimes, though, you need a job quickly to help make ends meet. And that's OK! Just keep in mind that if you find yourself unhappy at your job for whatever reason, you can always try to find a new one that fits better with your interests and skills. Besides, the connections you make at one job can help you find a better job down the road.

It's natural to be nervous as you search for your first job. The first time you do anything is stressful, and getting a job is a big step toward becoming an independent adult. Remember, no softball player hits a home run each time at bat, and no one has a 100 percent success rate in employment interviews. It's hard to be told no, especially for a job you're really excited about, but you only need one yes to start earning an income. Keep going, gain more skills, and don't sell yourself short! Eventually, you'll find that yes.

I wish you the best of luck in your search for your first job!

REBECCA

FORWARD

It may seem overwhelming at first to think about earning an income or finding a job, but these can be important steps toward living a healthy adult life. Now that you know what to focus on, you can pay it forward to a friend too. Remember the Get Healthy tips throughout this book, then take these steps to get healthy and get going.

1. Begin your job search by making a list of your interests, the skills you want to use and develop, and your ideal workplace. Use these characteristics to determine which of the potential jobs you identify is a good fit for you.

2. Look at the businesses around you for job opportunities, but also consider jobs that aren't as visible. The more open you are to different career options, the more likely the right job will end up on your list.

3. Don't talk yourself out of a great job before even applying for it. The worst a company can say is no.

4. Ask questions in the interview. Remember, every interview is a two-way street. The interviewer must want to hire you, but you also must want the job. Make sure it's a good fit for you.

5. Show up on the first day ready to learn. If you arrive with an open mind and ask questions, you'll be a valuable employee in no time.

6. Plan how you'll spend your money with a budget. A budget is a tool to ensure your money goes to the things you value most.

7. Get good at time management. Your first job will take up a lot of your free time. You'll need to be more efficient to finish all your schoolwork and household responsibilities in less time so you still have time for family and friends, relaxation, and sleep.

8. You have resources you can turn to if someone at the company makes you feel uncomfortable or threatens you. Make sure to document everything that happens and bring the information to your supervisor.

9. Be willing to re-evaluate your job. After you've held your first job for some time, consider whether your company and position are still good matches with your interests, the skills you want to use and develop, and your ideal work environment. If the circumstances have changed, begin researching alternatives.

GLOSSARY

adulting
A slang term for doing an activity that feels like it has an adult level of responsibility, such as creating a budget or paying taxes.

chamber of commerce
An association of business owners and employees that promotes commercial interests in the community.

cover letter
A letter accompanying a résumé sent to an employer by a job applicant. It explains the applicant's interest in the job, skills, and why the applicant would be successful in the position.

deduction
An amount of money withheld from an employee's paycheck, usually for income tax, social security, Medicare, or medical insurance payments.

Medicare
A US program that provides health-care coverage for people ages 65 and older.

reference

A person, such as a former manager or educator, who is asked during the hiring process to comment on a job applicant's skills and/or work ethic.

résumé

A document detailing a job applicant's academic achievements, awards, interests, work and volunteer experience, job skills, and other accomplishments.

seasonal job

A job that may be full-time or part-time but which only lasts for a limited duration. Summer, holiday, and busy-season jobs are seasonal jobs.

sexual harassment

Unwanted verbal or physical behavior that is sexual or gender based.

tax

Money that must be paid by law to the federal, state, or local government. A tax is frequently paid as a paycheck deduction.

ADDITIONAL
RESOURCES

SELECTED BIBLIOGRAPHY

Barreiro, Sachi. *Your Rights in the Workplace: An Employee's Guide to Fair Treatment*. NOLO, 2018.

Heilmann, Cara. *The Art of Finding the Job You Love*. Morgan James Publishing, 2018.

Mecham, Jesse. *You Need a Budget*. HarperBusiness, 2017.

FURTHER READINGS

Edwards, Sue Bradford. *Earning, Saving, and Investing*. Abdo, 2020.

Harris, Duchess, and Gail Radley. *Sexism at Work*. Abdo, 2018.

Harzog, Beverly Blair. *How Money Works: The Facts Visually Explained*. DK Publishing, 2017.

ONLINE RESOURCES

Booklinks
NONFICTION NETWORK
FREE! ONLINE NONFICTION RESOURCES

To learn more about earning an income, please visit **abdobooklinks.com** or scan this QR code. These links are routinely monitored and updated to provide the most current information available.

MORE INFORMATION

For more information on this subject, contact or visit the following organizations:

Boys and Girls Club of America

1275 Peachtree St. NE
Atlanta, GA 30309-3506
bgca.org/programs/career-development

The Boys and Girls Club of America has created career-development resources focused on building job skills and identifying career paths for teens.

Smart About Money

1331 Seventeenth St., Suite 1200
Denver, CO 80202
smartaboutmoney.org

Smart About Money is a program of the National Endowment for Financial Education, a nonprofit committed to educating people in the United States about financial topics.

YouthRules!

Wage and Hour Division
US Department of Labor
200 Constitution Ave. NW
Washington, DC 20210
youthrules.gov

YouthRules! is part of the US Department of Labor. It is an initiative that provides teens and young workers with information about jobs as well as resources to create safe workplace environments.

INDEX

ABOUT THE
AUTHOR

REBECCA J. ALLEN

Rebecca J. Allen writes middle-grade stories that blend mystery and adventure and young adult stories with heroines much braver than she is. She's the author of *Math Test Mischief* and *Showtime Sabotage*, both published under the pseudonym Verity Weaver. She's also a freelance writer of website and marketing content. She has a BA in economics from Wellesley College and an MBA from the Tuck School at Dartmouth College.